Young Entrepreneurs

Run Your Own
Bake Sale

Emma Carlson Berne

PowerKiDS press™

New York

Published in 2014 by The Rosen Publishing Group, Inc.
29 East 21st Street, New York, NY 10010

First Edition

Editor: Joanne Randolph
Book Design: Andrew Povolny
Photo Research: Katie Stryker

Photo Credits: Cover Maren Caruso/The Image Bank/Getty Images;pp. 5, 6 Hurst Photo/Shutterstock.com; p. 7 Cheryl Casey/Shutterstock.com; p. 9 CandyBox Images/Shutterstock.com; p. 10 Razmarinka/Shutterstock.com; p. 12 daniaphoto/Shutterstock.com; p. 13 iofoto/Shutterstock.com; p. 15 junpinzon/Shutterstock.com; p. 16 Andresr/Shutterstock.com; p. 17 istockphoto/Thinkstock; p. 18 Cavan Images/Taxi/Getty Images; p. 19 Diego Cervo/Shutterstock.com; p. 21 Monkey Business Images/Shutterstock.com; p. 22 kate_sept2004/E+/Getty Images; p. 25 Blend Images/Shutterstock.com; p. 26 XiXinXing/Getty Images; p. 28 Joe Polillio/Photographer's Choice/Getty Images; p. 29 Lisa Pines/The Image Bank/Getty Images.

Library of Congress Cataloging-in-Publication Data

Berne, Emma Carlson.
Run your own bake sale / by Emma Carlson Berne. — First edition.
    pages cm. — (Young entrepreneurs)
Includes index.
ISBN 978-1-4777-2918-2 (library) — ISBN 978-1-4777-3007-2 (pbk.) —
ISBN 978-1-4777-3078-2 (6-pack)
1. Money-making projects for children—Juvenile literature. 2. Selling—Juvenile literature. 3. Baked products—Juvenile literature. 4. Vending stands—Juvenile literature. 5. Entrepreneurship—Juvenile liteture. I. Title.
HF5392.B47 2014
664'.7520688—dc23
                                    2013022432
Manufactured in the United States of America

CPSIA Compliance Information: Batch #W14PK2: For Further Information contact Rosen Publishing, New York, New York at 1-800-237-9932

Contents

Your Very Own Business

Are you someone who comes up with fun solutions to problems? Are you the type of person who likes to make lists and plans? Do you like making your own money to buy things you want?

If you answered yes to these questions, then you might be a budding **entrepreneur**. An entrepreneur is a person who creates and organizes his own business.

You might think that a businessperson has to be an adult running a shop, restaurant, or large company. That is not true. Young people can be entrepreneurs, too.

There are six steps an entrepreneur will take when starting a business. First, she notices that there is a need for a **good** or **service**. When there is a need for something, this is called a **demand**. Then the entrepreneur will decide to start a business that will fulfill that need. This means she will create a **supply** of that good or service that meets the demand for it.

Adult entrepreneurs might decide to open a coffee shop, grocery store, or pizza place. They go through the same steps a young entrepreneur does. Every business starts with a good idea.

This young entrepreneur decided to start a dog-washing business in her neighborhood. Anyone with a good idea who is willing to do a little planning can start a business.

She will make a **business plan**. Then the entrepreneur starts the business. The job of an entrepreneur isn't done yet, though. She manages that business and makes the decisions about how it will run. Here's the best part. The entrepreneur collects the **profits**! This book will help you learn how to create and manage your very own business.

Big Decisions

The first thing you will need to decide is what kind of business you are going to start. The purpose of a business is to provide a product or service for people. Your business should fulfill a need or a want in your community.

Make a list of products or services you think you could provide. Then do some research. You can avoid competition by choosing a product that isn't already being provided.

A bake sale could be a great business for a young entrepreneur. Everyone likes to eat, so you have a built-in need already. You can sell your goodies at school or on the sidelines at sports games. The leftovers will be delicious, too!

Tip Central

If someone else is already providing the same business as you, you can make your own business more attractive to your customers by selling your products at a lower price than your competition.

Think about things you like to do or are good at. If you like baking with a parent and get lots of compliments on your chocolate cookies, you could turn that into a bake sale business.

9

Where, When, How?

Think about the ingredients you use when you bake, and make a list of those basic supplies.

To plan your bake sale, ask yourself these three questions: where, when, and how? First, where will you hold your bake sale? What are your different **venue** options? As a good entrepreneur, you'll want to pick a place where you will find a lot of hungry people. Is your school a good option? How about a sports game in your neighborhood or a street or church festival?

Once you decide on a venue, you'll want to get permission from the person in charge of that place, such as your principal. Most venues have rules about who can sell things and what they can sell. There may be a fee to use the space, too.

Choose simple recipes to make for your bake sale. It will take less time and cost less money to make recipes that do not require special ingredients and processes.

Ask a parent if you can use one of the kitchen drawers to store your measuring cups and other baking supplies so you always know where they are.

Next, decide when you want to hold your sale. Give yourself enough time to gather supplies and prepare your product. Then think about the times of day when people are hungry. Hungry people will buy more baked goods, and you will make more money.

Finally, think about how you will make your bake sale work. What will you need to purchase, rent, or borrow? Make a list of supplies. These will include the ingredients for the baked goods, plates, plastic wrap, and a table. Think about getting price stickers, a box for the cash, change, signs, and tape for the signs. A list will help you keep track of what you have and what you still need.

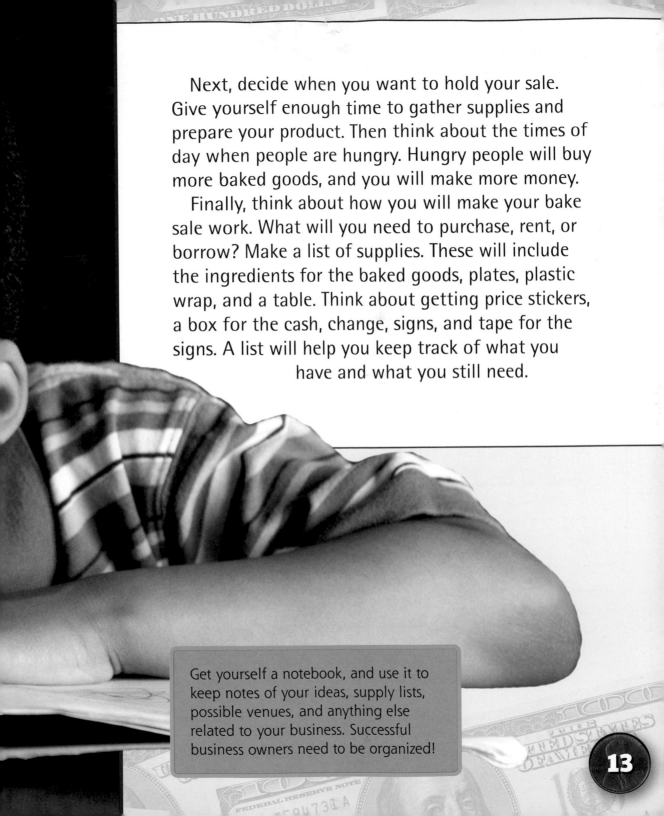

Get yourself a notebook, and use it to keep notes of your ideas, supply lists, possible venues, and anything else related to your business. Successful business owners need to be organized!

Money Out, Money In

Every business needs a **budget**. Your business's budget is a combination of how much money you will **invest**, or spend, on your business and how much **income** you expect to make from your business. To make a profit, you will need to earn more than you spend.

First, write down all of the things you will need to buy or rent for your bake sale. This is the money that you will need to spend on your business.

Tip Central

Always budget a little more money than you think you will need. Supplies may cost more than you originally thought, or you may have to buy something for which you didn't plan.

14

Count up how much money you have. Do you have enough to cover your start-up expenses? If not, you might think of ways to earn more money for your business or you could ask for a loan from your parents or an aunt or uncle.

Expense Budget	
Baking Supplies	$15.00
Cupcake Papers (50)	$5.00
Baggies (50)	$3.00
Total	**$23.00**

Your bake sale budget should include your expenses and your income. A spreadsheet can be a good way to keep track of costs and income. Here is a very basic sample of some of thing things you could include on your spreadsheet.

Next, think about where you will get this money. Do you have money saved? If you don't, you will have to go into **debt** by borrowing money, probably from your parents. When you borrow money from them, you will want to write down how much you are borrowing and when you will pay them back.

To help you budget, write down the costs for the baking supplies you will need the next time you are at the grocery store with your family.

Have a parent help you check your numbers. All successful businesses have to have good, sound budgets. Make sure you haven't forgotten any hidden expenses, such as the gas money you will owe a parent for driving you to buy supplies or to bake sales.

One way to avoid going into too much debt is to **estimate** your profits. This means you make an educated guess about how much money you think you will get out of your business. By making an estimate, you will be able to borrow the smallest amount possible.

It Pays to Advertise

Be sure to make your posters eye-catching but also easy to read.

Now that you have your business plan and your budget, it's time to think about advertising. It is a good idea to budget for the materials to make flyers and signs. This would include paper, markers, glue, or whatever else you need to make an eye-catching sign. You can distribute your flyers to your classmates or neighbors and post signs around your neighborhood or at school.

On your flyers and signs, be sure to mention where and when the bake sale will take place. Tell people why they should attend your bake sale, too. For example, you might write something like, "Hungry after school? Don't head home for your afternoon snack! Stop by Alex's After-School Bake Sale!"

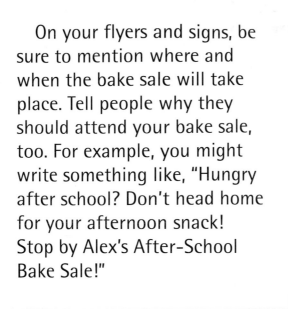

Tip Central

If your sale is taking place at school, ask your principal if you can make an announcement over the school's PA system. If you are selling at a sports game, ask the announcer to mention your sale during a break.

Think about placing an ad in your local newspaper. Some local newspapers will run an article about new businesses for free. Have a parent help you write an email to see if yours will do so.

People, Please!

Your bake sale will be fun, but there is a lot of work to be done, too. You might decide that having help will make things easier. You may need some **human resources**, or people to work with you in your business.

There are three areas in which you might need help. These are shopping for and baking your baked goods, setting up and taking down your sale, and the actual selling. Ask your friends if they want to be **employees**. If someone works for you, you will need to pay him. There are two ways you can pay employees. You can pay them flat fees. For example, you might pay your friend $10 for the whole time he is working for you.

If you work with a friend on the bake sale, you will have to decide if you will split your profits equally or if your friend will get a smaller amount than you.

You can also pay him hourly, maybe $5 for every hour he works. To figure out how much to pay, think about how much money you have been paid for babysitting or doing odd jobs for neighbors.

Remember that when you hire help, you will have to pay your employees out of the money you make. You might think that will mean you will make less money. Think about this, though. If you can hold a bigger bake sale because you have help, you may make more money overall.

Tip Central

Another way to get some help could be to let a friend have a table at your bake sale. She could pay you a fee for space at your venue to help cover all the advertising costs and legwork you have done. She can keep what she makes at her table, and you do not have to bake as many items yourself!

You could decide to hire your brother or sister to help you. This would make it easy to coordinate who is baking what since your employee lives in the same house as you!

Supply Yourself

It's time to buy or borrow your supplies. Buy carefully. If you buy too many supplies and don't use them all, you will have wasted money. This will cut into your profits.

First, examine the recipes you will use and make a list of ingredients to get at the grocery store. Make sure you have the right tools, like measuring spoons, cookie cutters, cupcake papers, and baking pans.

How will you display your baked goods? Will you use plates? Maybe you plan to bag and tie each baked good with ribbon individually? Either way, you'll need to make sure you have these things, as well as a marker or stickers to mark the prices.

It could be cheaper to buy some supplies online. Especially for supplies that you will need a lot of, such as paper plates, you might find a good deal online.

Tip Central

Ingredients like milk and eggs can spoil if they sit in your refrigerator for a long time. Don't buy these things too soon so you won't waste money.

Then, get some poster board, paper, markers, and tape for your advertising signs and flyers. You'll also need a large table and a container to hold the money you earn. Don't forget some coins and small bills, like ones and fives, to make change. You can get these from the bank.

Save the **receipts** from your purchases so you can add up how much money you've spent. Keep a list of everything you have borrowed, too, so you can make sure you return it all. Unless you live close enough to a store to ride your bike or walk, you will need to ask a grown-up to take you shopping. Be sure to ask politely and with enough advance notice that the grown-up can find the time to do this for you.

If your father takes you to the store, be sure to thank him and offer to help him do something around the house.

The Big Day Is Here!

On the day of your sale, pack your treats in containers and gather any tables or other supplies. Arrange a ride with a parent ahead of time if you can't get everything to the sale on your own.

It can make sense to add finishing touches at the bake sale site. Anything that might get ruined during travel can be done there. Be sure to leave enough time before your sale starts, though!

Make sure prices are clearly marked at your bake sale.

Start setting up about 1 to 2 hours before your sale. Tape a sign to the front of your table with the name of the bake sale and the hours.

Arrange your treats on their plates, or display them in their bags. If you can mark the prices before you go, do it. Otherwise, bring materials to mark the prices as you are setting up.

In a notebook, record each purchase and how much money was earned, such as "5 brownies x $1 per brownie = $5. When the sale is over, count the money you took in. Does the amount match the amount in your notebook?

Congratulations! You have successfully run your own bake sale. Now you can enjoy your profits!

Are You Ready?

On a separate sheet of paper, check off these items to make sure you have everything ready for your bake sale.

☐ Buy ingredients for baking. These might include flour, sugar, eggs, milk, chocolate chips, baking chocolate, butter, oil, and possibly cake or brownie mixes.

☐ Buy supplies for packaging and displaying the baked goods. These might include baggies, ribbon, and containers for carrying your baked goods to the venue.

☐ Buy supplies for posters and flyers. These should include tape, paper, and markers.

☐ Hang or distribute the posters and flyers.

☐ Buy labels or stickers for pricing and make a price list for yourself.

☐ Get a cash box.

☐ Go to a bank or ask a parent for change to go in the box. You'll want coins, ones, fives, and tens.

☐ Bake the baked goods.

☐ Pack the car with supplies for the sale the night before. Don't forget a table if your site will not supply one.

☐ Bring a notebook and pencil to record your sales.

☐ Bring a folder or envelope for receipts.

☐ Bring a calculator, just in case you need to check your math.

☐ Pack the baked goods.

☐ Head to the sale, set up, and have a great day!

Glossary

budget (BUH-jit) A plan to spend a certain amount of money in a period of time.

business plan (BIZ-nes PLAN) Something that lays out who will run a business, what it will sell, when and where it will sell it, and how it will be set up and run.

debt (DET) Something owed.

demand (dih-MAND) A need or want people have for a good or a service.

employees (im-ploy-EEZ) People who are paid to work for a person or a business.

entrepreneur (on-truh-pruh-NUR) A businessperson who has started his or her own business.

estimate (ES-teh-mayt) To make a guess based on knowledge or facts.

good (GUD) A product sold to others.

human resources (HYOO-mun REE-sors-ez) The efforts of people who make goods and provide services.

income (IN-kum) Money received for work.

invest (in-VEST) To put money into something, such as a company, in the hope of getting more money later on.

profits (PRAH-fits) The money a company makes after all its bills are paid.

receipts (rih-SEETS) Slips of paper that note how much was paid for a certain item and where and when it was bought.

service (SIR-vis) Something that a person does for other people.

supply (suh-PLY) The amount of goods or services available.

venue (VEN-yoo) The place where a business is located.

Index

Websites

Due to the changing nature of Internet links, PowerKids Press has developed an online list of websites related to the subject of this book. This site is updated regularly. Please use this link to access the list:
www.powerkidslinks.com/ye/bake/